PLEASE **TREAT** THIS BOOK WITH **RESPECT**

GURU TEGH BAHADUR JI

Love Compassion Righteousness

Author & Illustrator
Ishpal Kaur

1621 - 1675
GURU TEGH BAHADUR JI
Ninth Master, Ninth Guru Ji

Guruship
1664 - 1675
Guru Tegh Bahadur Ji
Ninth Guru Nanak Dev Ji
Guru Nanak Dev Ji's light...
Guru Tegh Bahadur Ji
The Sikh's ninth Guru Ji...
The putar (son) of our sixth Guru Ji
The chacha (uncle) of our seventh Guru Ji
The baba (grandfather) of our eighth Guru Ji
The pita (father) of our tenth Guru Ji
The ongoing Joth (divine light) of our first Guru Ji...
The ongoing Joth (divine light), of all our Guru Ji's.

Before Guruship....

01

Guru Tegh Bahadur Ji was born in Amritsar, 1621, to Mata Nanaki Ji and Guru Hargobind Ji (the Sikh's sixth Guru Ji). During their childhood in Amritsar, Guru Ji was educated in a range of languages from, Bhai Gurdas Ji, whilst their martial training was taught by both, Baba Buddha Ji and their father, Guru Hargobind Ji.

02

Guru Tegh Bahadur Ji confidently used their swordsman martial skills to fight the Kartarpur battle during their early youth. Guru Tegh Bahadur Ji's original name was 'Tyag Maal' - renouncer of all, but as Guru Ji fought so valiantly, after winning the battle they were renamed 'Tegh Bahadur' - best swordsman. Guru Ji was very studious, but they would also spend a lot of their time in deep meditation.

03

Later, Guru Ji was wedded to Mata Gujari Ji. Guru Ji eventually relocated with Mata Gujari Ji and Mata Nanaki Ji to a modest secluded room in their maternal village, Bakala. It was here where Guru Ji spent several years in deep meditation.

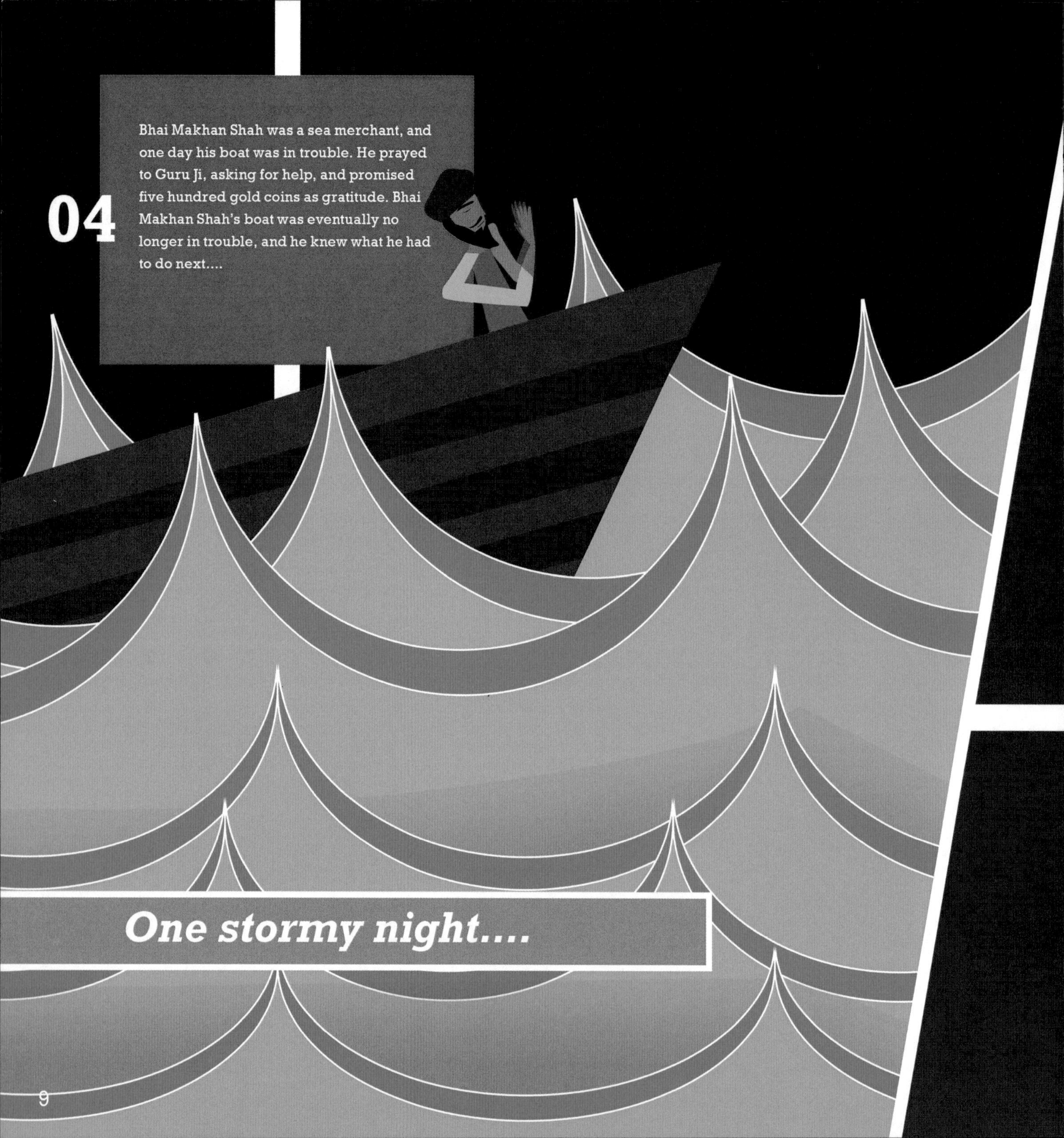
04
Bhai Makhan Shah was a sea merchant, and one day his boat was in trouble. He prayed to Guru Ji, asking for help, and promised five hundred gold coins as gratitude. Bhai Makhan Shah's boat was eventually no longer in trouble, and he knew what he had to do next....
One stormy night....

Guru Tegh Bahadur Ji

Ninth Guru Nanak Dev Ji

1664, Guruship Began....

05

They set off to go to Delhi to see the Sikh's Guru Ji, Guru Sri Harkrishan Ji (eighth Guru Ji), but were informed that they had left this world and had spoken of the next Guru Ji... 'Baba Bakala'. Bhai Makhan Shah then set off to the village Bakala, in search of the next Guru Ji. Seeing many people 'claiming' to be Guru, he tested them with offering only two gold coins. When reaching Guru Tegh Bahadur Ji, again he offered two gold coins only, but Guru Ji knew and asked where the five hundred gold coins were that they had promised. Guru Ji was not at all greedy, but Guru Ji knew that they were being tested, and did not want Bhai Makhan Shah to go disappointed.

...The next Guru Ji, was finally found.

After Guruship....

01

After attaining the responsibility of the next Guruship, Guru Tegh Bahadur Ji went on to travel around India, spreading the message of Guru Nanak Dev Ji, bringing people's relationship with Vaheguru Ji closer with the enlightening Gurbani.

02

Whilst on their travels, Guru Ji had purchased some land, which was then constructed into Chakk Nanaki (later known as Anandpur Sahib). Guru Ji reached Patna in 1666, when Mata Gujari was also expecting their first child. That same year, Mata Nanaki helped deliver the blessed arrival of her grandson, Gobind Rai Ji.

03

The first few years of Gobind Rai Ji's childhood were spent in Patna until Guru Ji came back from their travels. They then relocated to the new city of Anandpur Sahib. It was there where Gobind Rai Ji became learned in many languages including Gurmukhi, Sanskrit, Braj and Persian. Gobind Rai Ji also showed a keen interest in many martial disciplines at a young age and were very well skilled in them too. In 1675, things were about to change for Gobind Rai Ji and their father, Guru Tegh Bahadur Ji.

Vaheguru
Vaheguru

Religious Discrimination....

01

For some time, the Mughals were reigning over areas of India. During this time of reign, religious conversion or otherwise exploitation, was an occurring problem in India.

02

Not all the Kings during the Mughal Empire imposed the radical idea of wanting to convert everybody to Islam, however, some did, and this time it was the Mughal King, Aurangzeb.

03

The notion was, all shall be one religion otherwise, exploit and threaten, until either they change their mind, or die.

....

Exploitation

Discrimination

Inequality

Discrimination

Inequality

Exploitation

Inequality

Discrimination

Inequality

Exploitation Inequality

Exploitation

Discrimination

Exploitation

Inequality

CHANGE YOUR
RELIGION, OR...
DEATH!

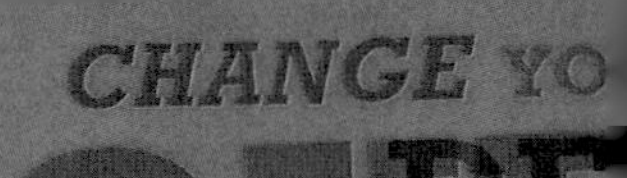

CHANGE YOUR RELIGION, OR DEATH!

Guru Ji's Helping Hand....

01

The Kashmiri Pandits were being threatened by the Kashmiri Governor at the time. Cruel atrocities were being inflicted on the people. The Kashmiri Pandits had been threatened to either convert to Islam or die. The notion was that if they could convert the Brahmin Kashmiri Pandits, the Hindu Priests, then thousands of others would convert as a result. The Kashmiri Pandits then went to Guru Tegh Bahadur Ji and told Guru Ji about the unjustly and unrighteous situation that they were faced with, and graciously asked for their help.

Equality & Justice
The Helping Soul....

Guru Tegh Bahadur Ji was a kind soul and loved Vaheguru Ji. Their mind was in a complete meditative state, absorbed and united with Vaheguru Ji. Guru Ji was a devotee of the 'One' the creator of the universe, and it was their duty to help those in need.

The Next Guru Ji...

01

Guru Tegh Bahadur Ji said it is time for someone noble to make a sacrifice. Gobind Rai Ji found out about the dilemma that the Kashmiri Pandits were in and heard their father's suggestion. Gobind Rai Ji then said that there is no other noble man in this world such as yourself father, that can give their life to help the people against this injustice. Upon hearing Gobind Rai Ji's proposal and willingness to sacrifice their father for the better good, Guru Ji was pleased with their young son's response.

02

Guru Ji accepted the proposition, and the Mughal Empire were then notified that if they could convert Guru Tegh Bahadur Ji then all will accept Islam. Guru Ji decided that Gobind Rai Ji was also ready for the Guruship, Guru Nanak Dev Ji's humble seat. In 1675, Gobind Rai Ji who was only nine years old at the time, became the tenth Guru for the Sikhs and was then known as, **'Guru Gobind Rai Ji'.**

Guru Gobind Rai Ji
Tenth Ongoing Light Of Guru Nanak Dev Ji
1675, Guruship Began....

The Arrest....

01

Later, Guru Tegh Bahadur Ji left Anandpur Sahib to travel to Delhi, and with them were five other sevadaars (devotees). During their travels, Guru Ji and the five devotees that were alongside them, were arrested by the Mughal authorities.

02

Guru Tegh Bahadur Ji and the five devotees were accompanied by 400 Mughals for the remaining journey to Delhi. Aurangzeb had a warrant to find Guru Ji, but Guru Ji already knew everything. The unwavering Guru Tegh Bahadur Ji, and three of the devotees that had been arrested, were all eventually imprisoned.

The Next Guru Ji....
It was during Guru Ji's time in prison that they wrote a letter to Gobind Rai Ji. After Gobind Rai Ji's reply to the letter, Guru Ji arranged for the Guruship ceremony of Gobind Rai Ji's to take place.
The conversation that took place between Guru Tegh Bahadur Ji and Gobind Rai Ji was included in Sri Guru Granth Sahib Ji.

They were all...
arrested....

It was November...

DELHI,

1675

Chandni Chowk, ***Delhi....***

The Shaheeds....

01 The devotees, Bhai Sati Daas, Bhai Mati Daas and Bhai Dayala Ji, served the Guru's house, the house of Guru Nanak Dev Ji. Their love and devotion for Guru Tegh Bahadur Ji was unwavering.

02 All three devotees were tortured in front of Guru Ji, as the Mughals wanted to see if Guru Tegh Bahadur Ji would waver. To the Mughals dismay, Guru Ji was steadfast in their beliefs, and each devotee lovingly gave their life for their Guru Ji.

Shaheedi: **Delhi, 1675**

03

Guru Tegh Bahadur Ji were not afraid of death, and they were not going to waver on their faith and convert. Guru Ji was making a sacrifice for mankind. This was the will, of Vaheguru Ji.

04

Aurangzeb ordered for Guru Ji to be beheaded. It is said that Aurangzeb had asked Guru Ji as to why their name was 'Tegh Bahadur'. Guru Ji told Aurangzeb that during the execution ceremony, you will come to realise the meaning of my name.

Guru Tegh Bahadur Ji

was in a state of,

TRUE

ANAND!

bliss....

And then....

Japji Sahib paath
Before leaving their mortal clay body, Guru Tegh Bahadur Ji recited Japji Sahib paath.

Ik...
Oangkaar....

Guru Ji's Shaheedi....

01

Guru Tegh Bahadur Ji was ready to give their sees (head). After drinking some water from the prison well, Guru Ji also took an ishaan (bath) and then sat by the tree nearby. In complete concentration, Guru Ji began to recite Japji Sahib paath (Sikh prayer).

02

After finishing reciting the paath, Guru Ji then bowed in reverence to Guru Sahib. The executioner was ready to commence.

03

Bhai Jaitha Ji was one of the sevadaars (devotees) that had accompanied Guru Tegh Bahadur Ji. As the executioner rose his tegh (sword) and swung with all his might, Bhai Jaitha Ji's hands were ready to receive Guru Ji's pavitra (pure) sees.

04

Guru Ji told them that no sword can take their head. Just as the blow of strike was going to happen, Guru Tegh Bahadur Ji, the greatest swordsman, gave their head themselves. Guru Ji's sees fell into the arms of Bhai Jaitha Ji. The executioner was in shock and feared what he had witnessed. The paper and thread that had been wrapped around the sword was still intact, showing to the world that no sword took Guru Ji's head...Guru Ji, gave their head.

...Guru Ji, **gave** their **head.**

Vaheguru....

Guru Ji's Sees (Head)
Guru Tegh Bahadur Ji gave their head, but not their faith.

Guru Ji's Arrival
Guru Gobind Rai Ji welcomed Bhai Jaitha Ji who bravely brought Guru Tegh Bahadur Ji's sees.

Guru Gobind Rai Ji
Guru Gobind Rai Ji received their father's sees and knew what had to be done next.

Noble Sacrifice
Bhai Jaitha Ji eventually became, Bhai Jivan Singh Ji.

Guru Ji

01

Bhai Jaitha Ji travelled cautiously to Anandpur Sahib to meet Guru Gobind Rai Ji so they could respectfully give them their father's sees. Guru Ji was pleased by the courageous act of Bhai Jaitha Ji and called them, 'Rangreta, Guru Ka Bheta' (Guru Ji's child).

02

After Guru Ji gave their sees, many were afraid to take Guru Ji's pavitar (pure) body, including even devotees of Guru Ji. During the current Mughal Empire, many atrocities were inflicted on the people and caused fear in many hearts. However, a huge storm had come about after Guru Ji's Shaheedi. Bhai Lakhi Shah Ji used this opportunity and took Guru Ji's body. He performed Guru Tegh Bahadur Ji's last rites by burning down his entire house, so the Mughals would not suspect the cremation of Guru Ji's pavitar (pure) body.

Going Home to Vaheguru Ji

Guru Ji left their mortal clay body, but their soul...
lived on forever, with Vaheguru Ji.

Degh Tegh Fateh
Food Protection Victory

Degh Tegh Fateh,
Degh; food is important for our body,
Humanity is to help serve others that are in need,
Langar is free food that is welcome to everybody.

Degh is what we need,
Some have it at ease, whilst others do struggle,
Having the sense of humanity and compassion,
With the concept of Degh, we can try to help all.

Degh, Tegh, Fateh,
Tegh; protection is our duty,
As oppression and injustice is not what we stand for,
And our purpose is to end tyranny.

Tegh; we should not let ourselves be mistreated,
Neither should others be condemned to unrighteous acts,
When the truth is there, but unseen because of ignorance,
Through love, compassion and justice, we can overcome such.

Degh, Tegh, Fateh,
Fateh; the victory,
The victory against injustice and oppression,
The victory of endless love, in this world story.

Fateh is the victory of equality,
The victory of eternal peace,
The victory of living freely,
The victory of living together, with ease.

Sarbat Da Bhala
Blessings For Everyone

From 'One' came all,
From all to 'One',
There are many directions,
But the destination is still, 'One'.

Stay strong within yourself,
Within your belief,
No one is higher or lower,
But never waver, on your belief.

Dedication and devotion, for the search for the 'One',
For on our journey there are many you may meet,
Humanity is to be instilled within our hearts,
Compassion, righteousness, justice will prevail, whilst evil will defeat.

All the things that pull us away from thinking clearly,
And then not knowing how to act, not knowing what to say,
But if we always keep in mind our Guru Ji's teachings, and Vaheguru Ji's name,
Their name will resonate inside us, every single day.

Their name is our strength and support,
Their name is our boat to sail across the shore,
From Their name all our affairs can be resolved,
The 'One' who is inside of us all, and who loves us forever more.

Blessed, blessed is our Guru Tegh Bahadur Ji,
Who loved their faith dearly,
Who wished good for everyone,
That they gave their life, but not their love for ***Vaheguru Ji.***

Guru Tegh Bahadur Ji

The Ninth Master for the Sikhs...
Is Guru Tegh Bahadur Ji,
Valiant swordsman, fearless warrior,
Yet unattached and patient as could be.

Our beautiful noble...
Guru Tegh Bahadur Ji,
With their brave and kind soul,
Gave their head, for the sake of humanity.

Cries of many disturbed souls from the oppression...
From the cruel actions of religious exploitation,
Threats and forced conversion,
Death, or change your religion!

The saddened souls, the Kashmiri Pandits...
Went to Guru Tegh Bahadur Ji,
Crying for shelter and guidance,
Humbly asked, to please help stop this misery.

Guru Gobind Singh Ji, Guru Gobind Rai Ji at the time...
Came to hear of this situation,
'One noble man should give his life'
'If you can change me, then change everyone's religion'....

'There is no other noble soul'...
'Who can go through this execution'
Guru Tegh Bahadur Ji was not to waver,
So, changing Guru Ji, was an impossible mission.

After Gobind Rai Ji spoke and said such words...
Guru Ji accepted to give their life,
As Guru Ji was neither to change,
Or go without helping anyone in strife.

Guru Ji realised that Gobind Rai Ji was ready...
Ready and deserving of the next Guruship,
After willing to sacrifice their father for others,
From the tyranny and oppressive hardship.

Guru Ji was arrested and then imprisoned...
But they could not change our Guru Ji,
They were fighting...for the freedom of faith,
Our beloved, Guru Tegh Bahadur Ji.

Our Ninth Master...
Our Guru Tegh Bahadur Ji,
Without any hesitation,
Gave their head so humbly.

Tyag Maal, renouncer of all...
Guru Ji's original name,
So true were their character,
So true, were They.

Seeing from the heavens whilst Guru Ji was going to give their head...
Rose cheers of joy...for Guru Ji's victory, and soon arrival,
Whilst the people on Earth, cried with woe,
As Guru Ji gave their life, for another faith's survival.

OUR **GURU JI**
NINTH **MASTER**

1) Do you know the ***name*** of the ninth Master?

2) *Where* was the ninth Master born?

3) Do you know ***when*** the ninth Master was born?

BEFORE **1664**
BEFORE **GURUSHIP**

1) Where did Guru Ji ***relocate*** after marriage?

2) *Who* went with Guru Ji?

3) *What* did Guru Ji do for several years?

AFTER **1664**
AFTER **GURUSHIP**

1) *How* did Guru Ji become the ninth Guru Ji?

2) *Why* did Guru Ji go travelling?

3) *Where* had Guru Ji arrived in 1666?

GOBIND **RAI JI**
GURU JI'S **SON**

1) What ***year*** was Gobind Rai Ji born?

2) Who helped ***deliver*** Gobind Rai Ji?

3) *What* was Gobind Rai Ji's mother's name?

KASHMIRI **PANDITS**
THE **EXPLOITED**

1) Why were the Kashmiri Pandits troubled?

2) *How* did the Kashmiri Pandits feel?

3) *Who* did the Kashmiri Pandits ask for help?

DELHI **1675**
THE **SACRIFICE**

1) *Who* was arrested in Delhi in 1675?

2) *Why* were they arrested?

3) *What* happened after they had been arrested?

Author & Illustrator
Ishpal Kaur

Made in the USA
Coppell, TX
02 May 2023